THE WILL TO LIVE...THE COURAGE TO LOVE

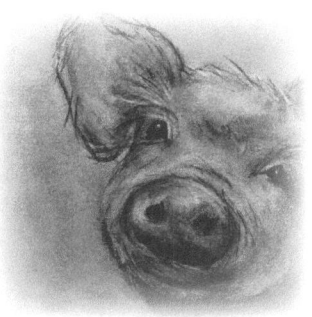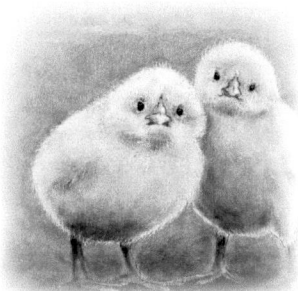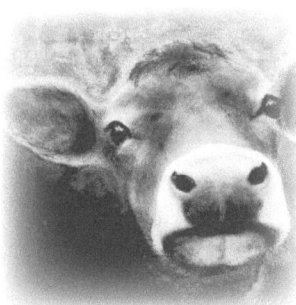

Sanctuary

BY JODY SIMS

ISBN-978-0-692-92905-6

Sanctuary sanc•tu•ar•y *(noun)*
a place of refuge or safety
In its original meaning, it is a sacred place.

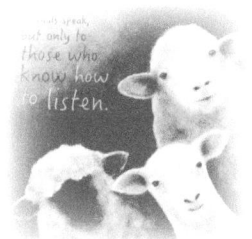

...als speak, but only to those who know how to listen.

"What feels like the end . . . is often the beginning."

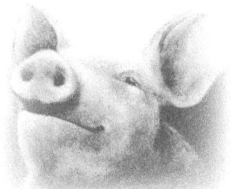

The will to live . . .

I had cancer, stage three. Susanne, my spouse, was rear-ended by a semi and suffered a traumatic brain injury. We were alive, but over time, we were still struggling to survive.

Our challenges were many . . . physical, emotional, financial, spiritual. We could no longer afford to live the way we once had or physically do the things we used to do. Ultimately, there was no choice but to move away from the people we loved and the place we called home.

Twenty-two hundred miles away, from California to east Tennessee, we settled into a quaint house with a dreamy screened-in porch (perfect for afternoon naps) and a yard just big enough for a garden. In the back, we built a shed and turned it into an art studio. One by one we met our neighbors, who made us feel welcomed and safe.

Sounds idylic, right?

It was . . . except for the fact that I couldn't seem to let my heart love our new world. It just didn't feel anything like the life we had before all the bad stuff happened. I longed for my old life. Honestly, there were days when I struggled to find the will to live.

I had an awakening...

One day, I read in the paper about a cow who was missing a foot and the people who were trying to help him. His name was Dudley, and he was having a prosthesis made for him at the University of Tennessee, just minutes from where we now lived.

Miraculously, the story of Dudley's plight found its way to the folks at the Gentle Barn in California. Rather than taking him all the way to the west coast to live out his life, they opened the Gentle Barn Tennessee – a sanctuary for abused farm animals.

Drawn to his story, Susanne and I went to meet Dudley as soon as we could. It turned out to be a day that would change our lives dramatically. She began volunteering there, and it wasn't long before I saw her spirits lift – her anxiety and despair replaced by joy and a sense of peace.

Through Susanne's experience and from meeting and learning how, like us, each animal had survived against tremendous odds . . .
I had an awakening!

I awoke to a deeper understanding of what it means to survive; how a heart opens up to compassion for all sentient beings; how my choices make a difference; and why sanctuary is key to finding the will to live.

This is what I heard . . .

As is so often the case when you open your heart . . . life started to unfold and seemingly begin again. I became a vegan, my energy came back, I started to meet people, ideas began to flow, and I found myself sitting in front of my easel, ready to paint.

When one of our new friends asked me if I'd like to hang some of my art in a restaurant she was opening, I took it as a sign. Her restaurant was going to be called **Sanctuary** Vegan Cafe! I knew immediately what I wanted to paint – rescued farm animals. I wanted to try to give them a voice . . . show the world how they are no different from us . . . give a glimpse of who they really are.

For the next several months, I retreated to my studio. What came out of my inward retreat was a new series of art I called "Compassion Makes Life Beautiful." The paintings (portraits) were inspired by many of the animals I met face to face, but some of them I had only read about.

As I painted each one . . . spending hours, often days bringing their images to life . . . I tried to imagine what the animals would say if they could speak. I found myself "listening" to them.

This is what I heard . . .

"I never saw the sun or smelled fresh air.
No one knew my name. Then one day, a lady
came and took me into her arms. She gave me
a name and a place to call home. Now I run
and play and get my belly rubbed."

Mercy

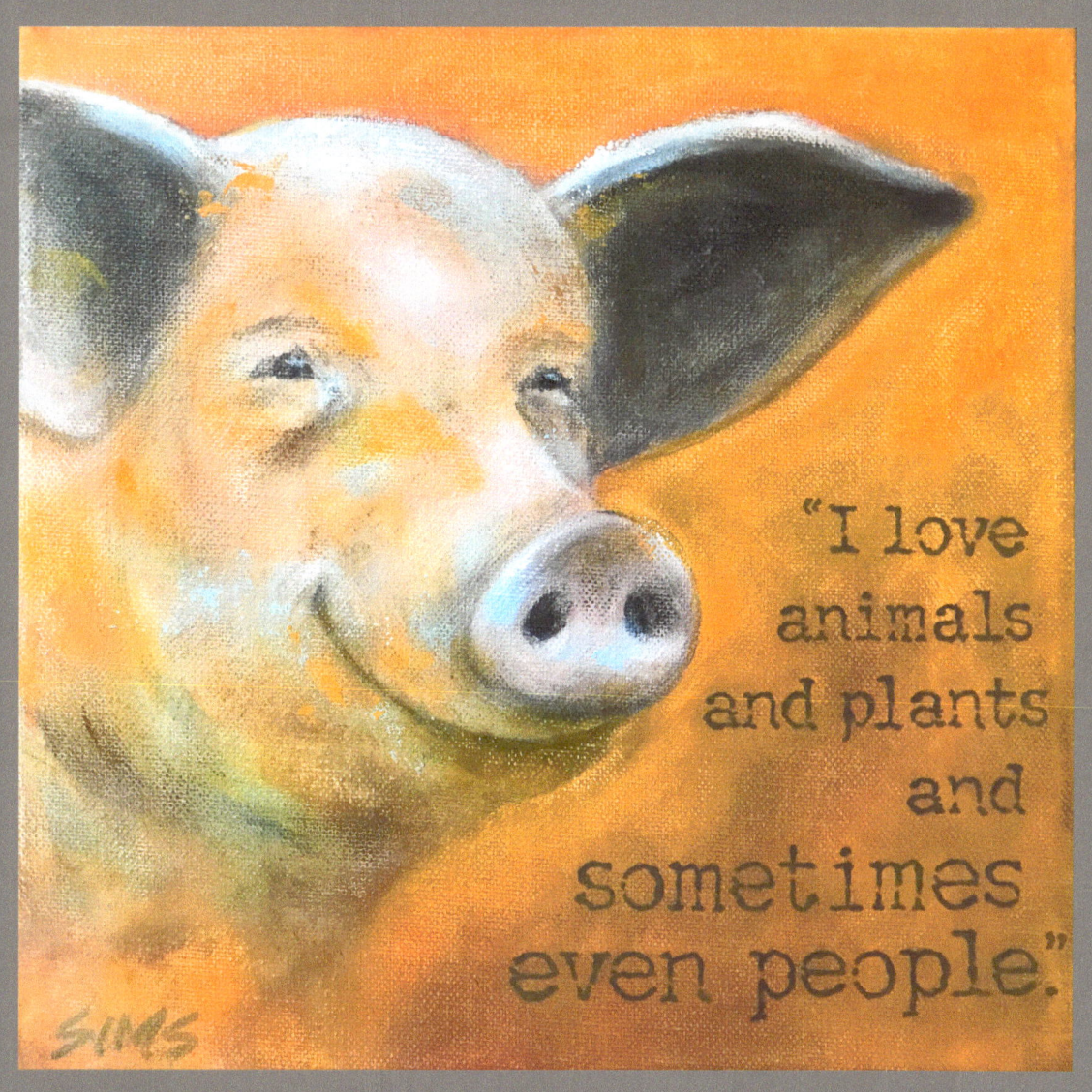

"I love animals and plants and sometimes even people."

SIMS

"I am old and now I'm here. My new home is filled with smiling faces and gentle hands that remind me I am loved. Kindness feels amazing."

Empathy

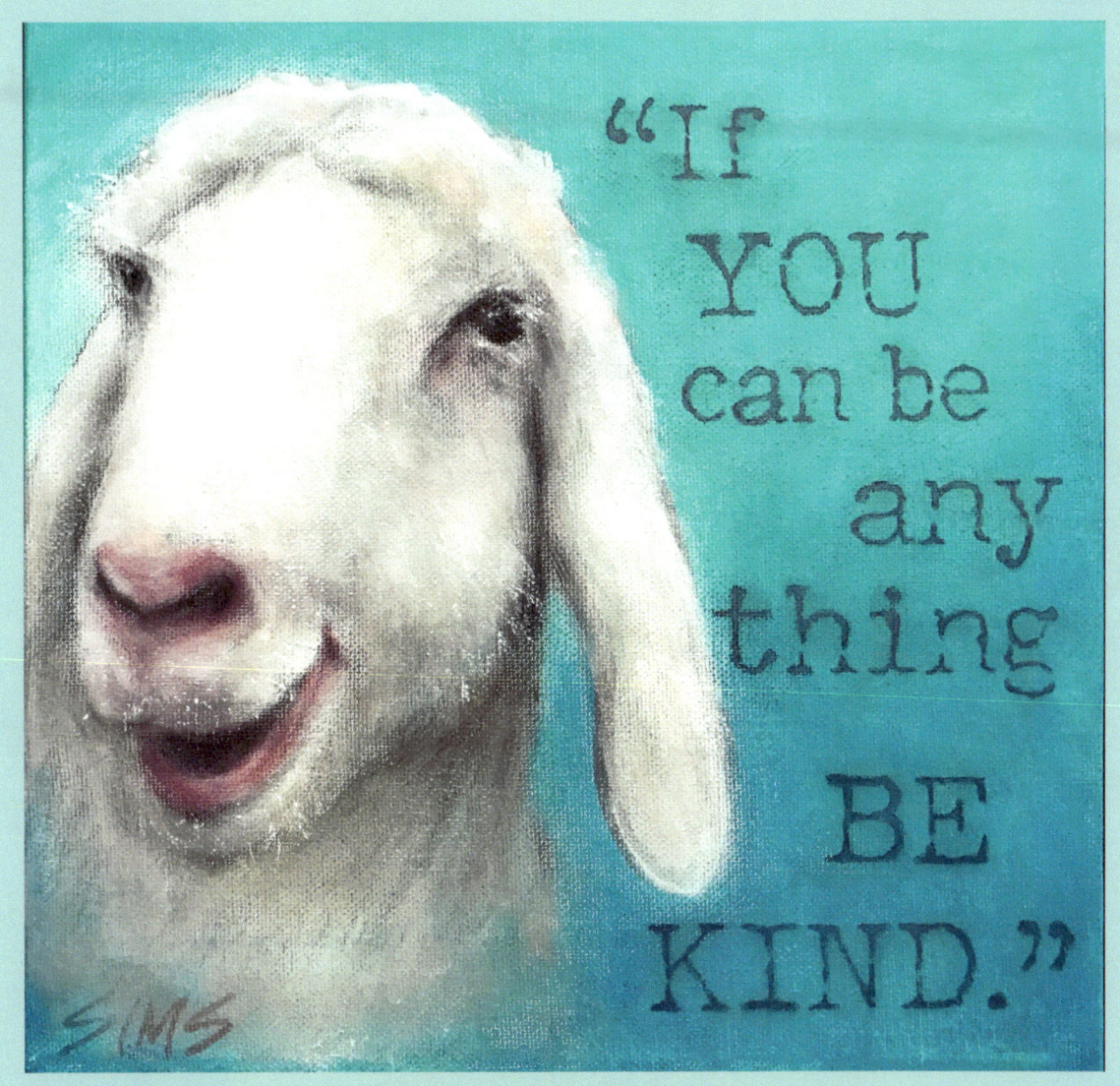

"The feathers on my tail are a very dark brown. The top of my head is a crazy shade of blue. My best friend has deep purple feathers on her tail, and the top of her head is pink. We do not look the same, and that is what makes us beautiful."

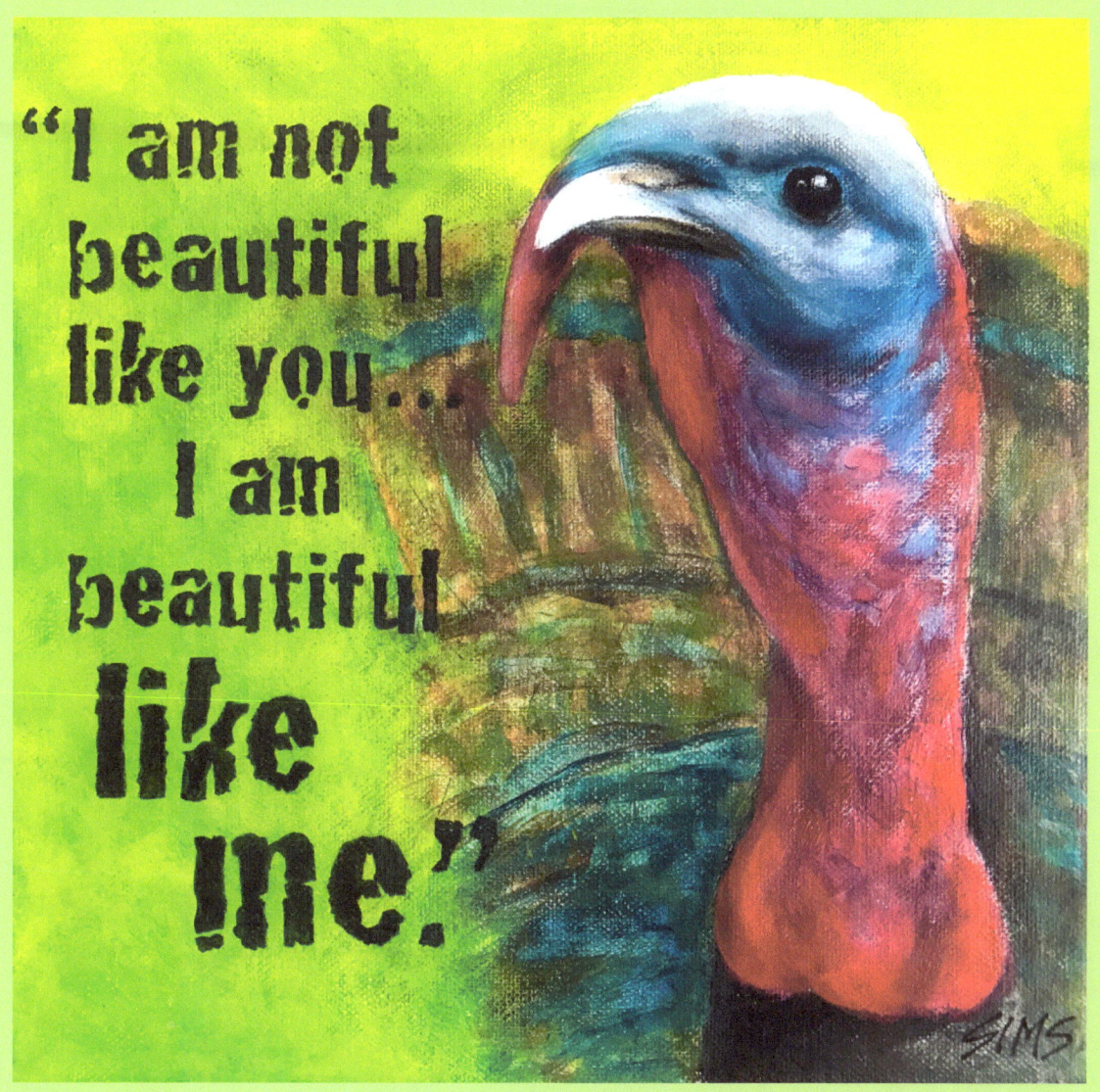

"I am not beautiful like you... I am beautiful like me."

"I made a new friend today! As I was headed to my favorite mud hole, I met this cat who could not walk across the mud without getting stuck, so I gave him a ride. It feels good to help others."

Charity

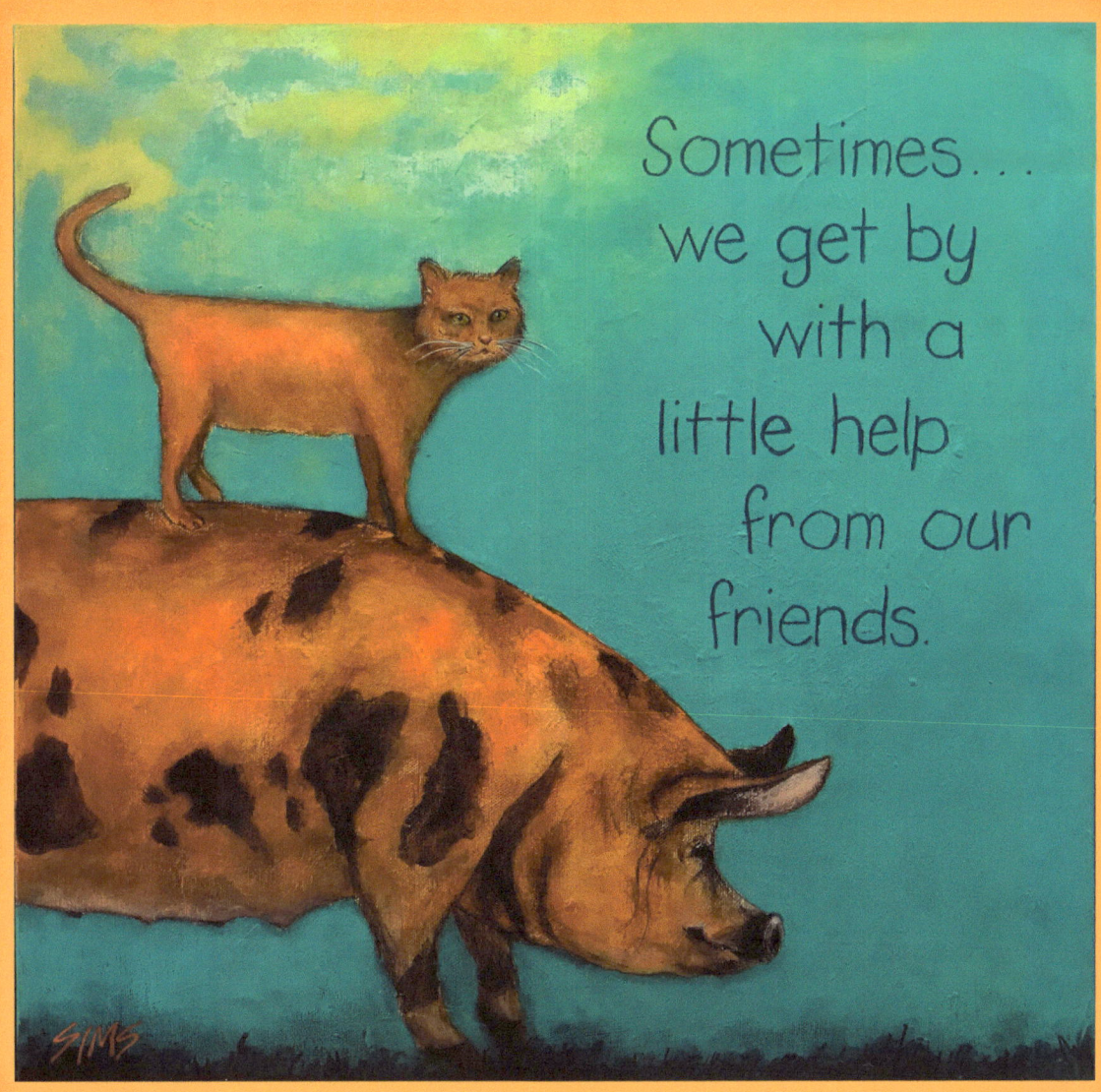

"You may not think we talk, but we do!
All we ask is that you get really quiet,
look into our eyes . . . and listen."

Believe

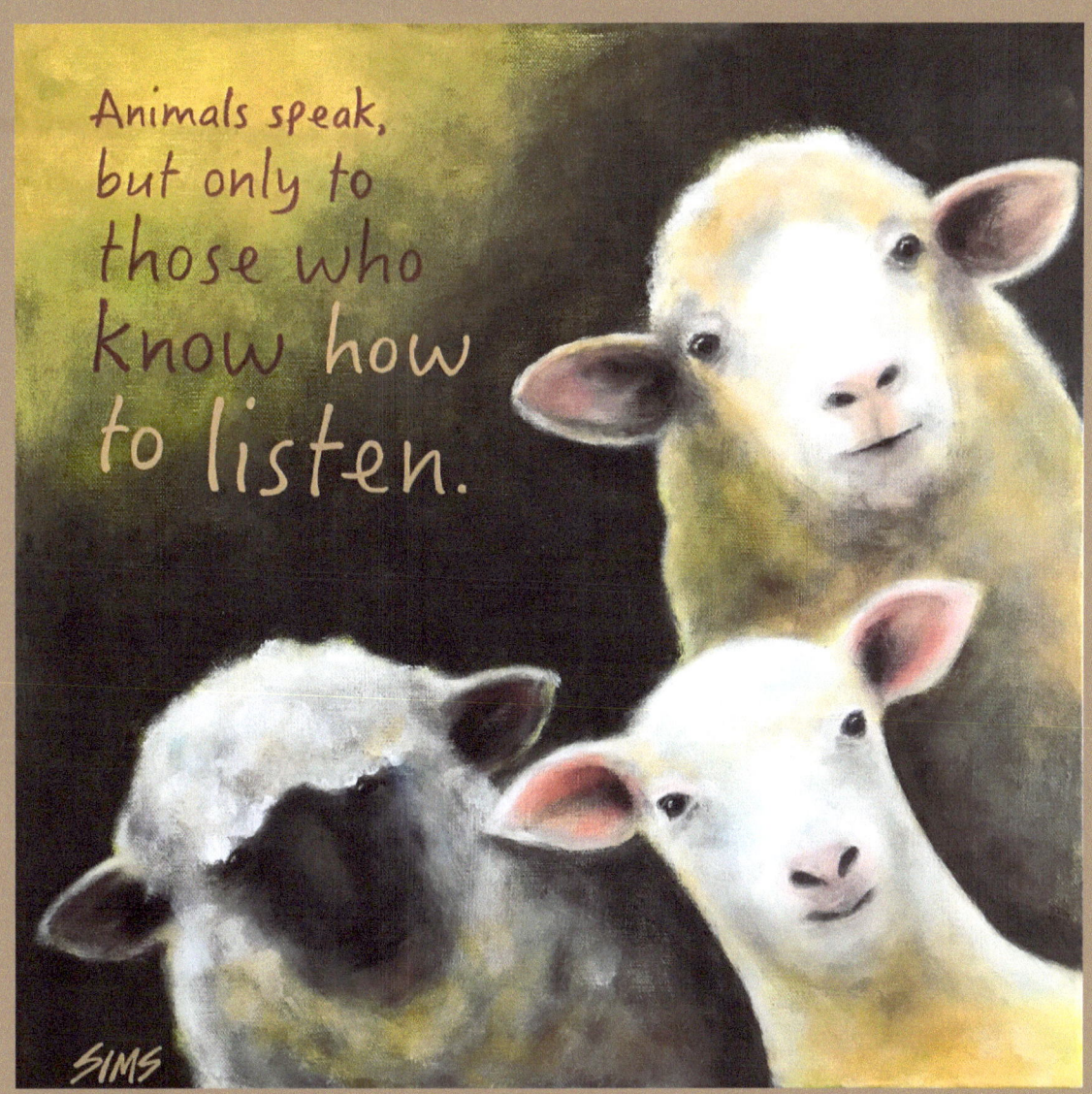

"Living here, I have begun to learn others'
languages. Somehow, this makes me feel taller!
Do you talk pig? Did you know that when I
oink (or groink) really loudly, I am scared?
But if I oink quietly or softly I might just want
my belly rubbed! And just so you know . . .
my quiet 'panting sound' is my way of saying
'hello' or maybe even 'I love you.'"

Confidence

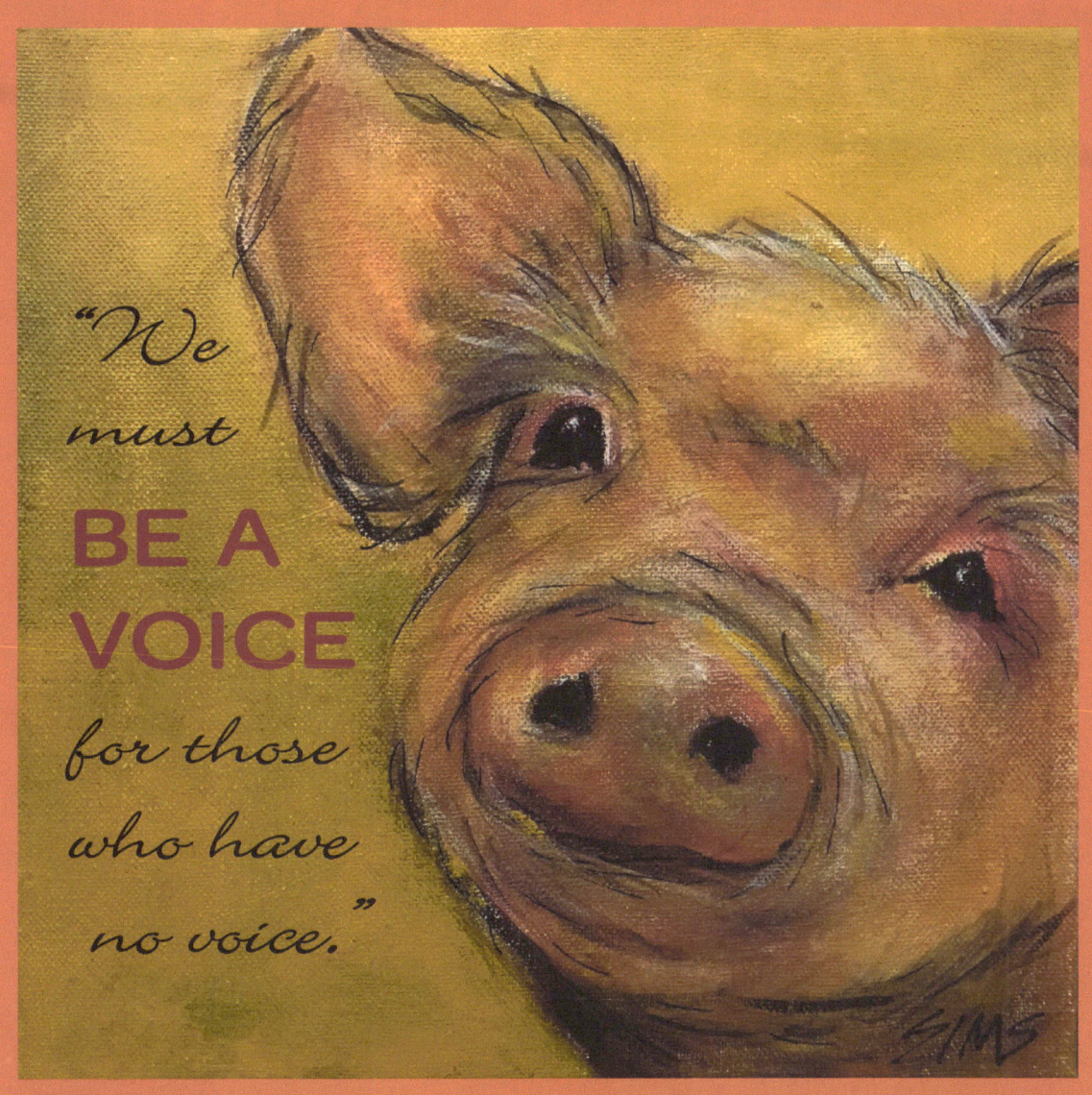

"We must **BE A VOICE** for those who have no voice."

"Do you have a pet? I have a cat! Even though I'm a cow, I love my little friend. We enjoy hanging out together, taking naps, and sometimes playing hide and seek. If he hides behind my back hoof, I can't find him!"

Friendship

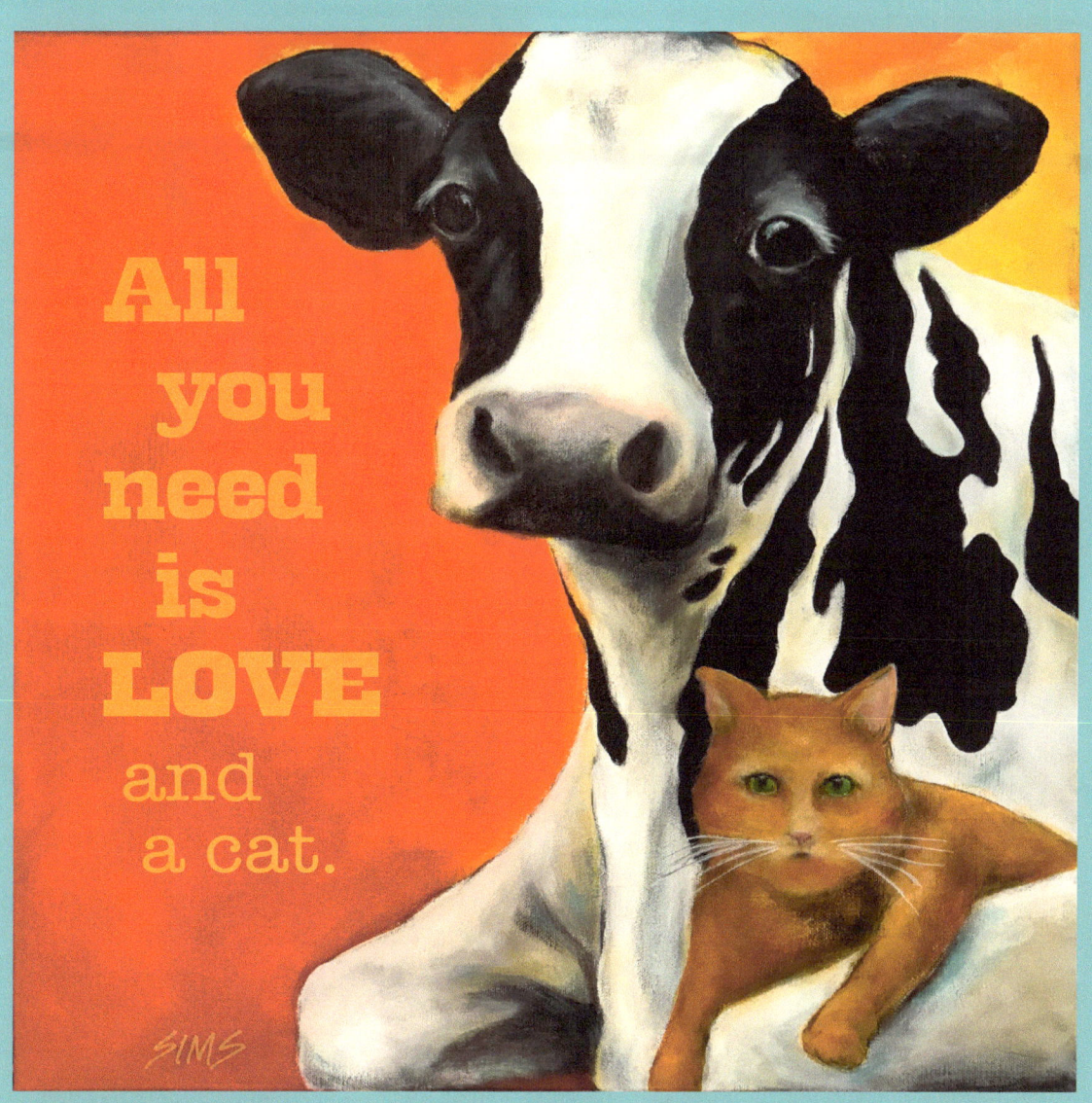

"Everyone and everything is SO big.
We see you . . . and we hope that you see us."

Connect

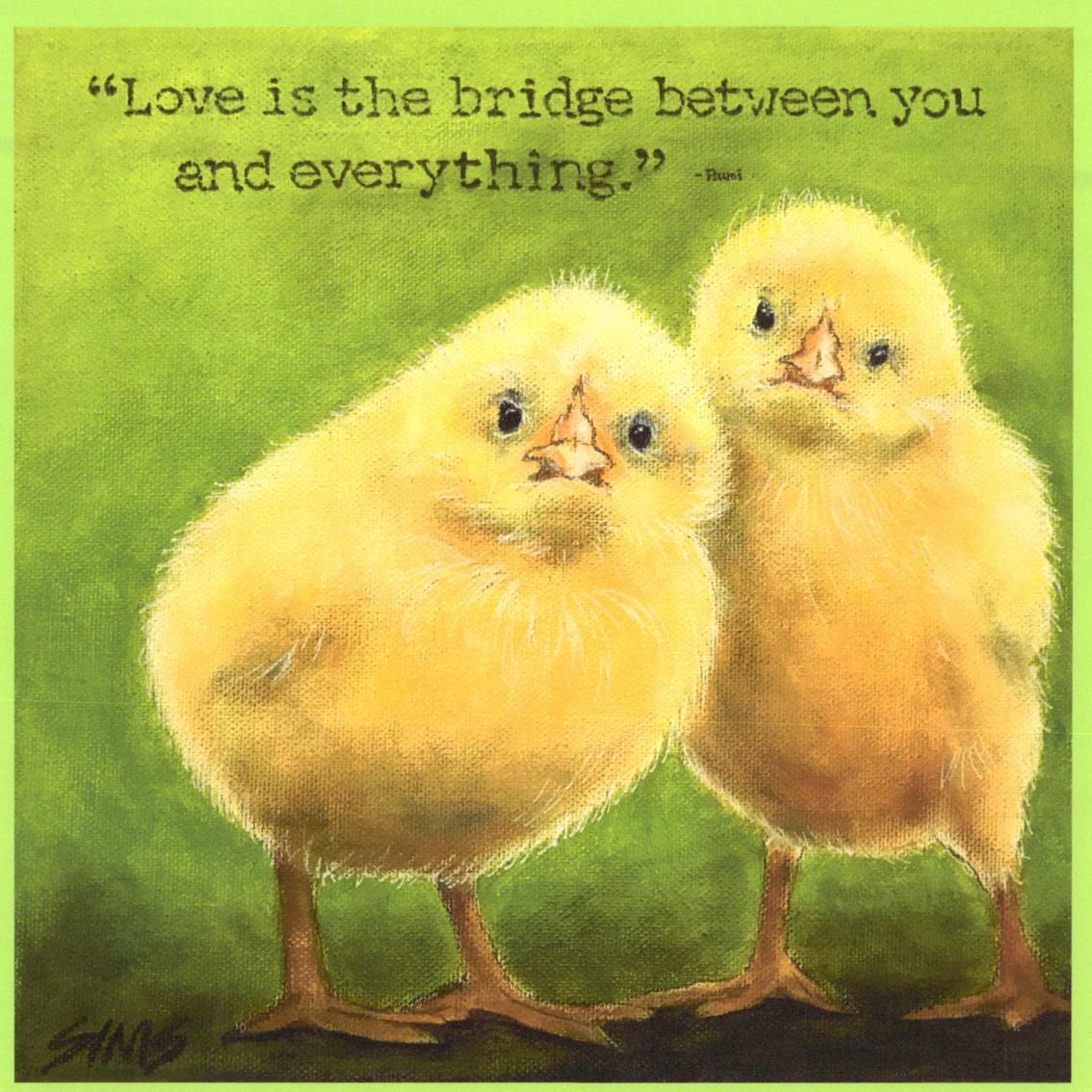

"I used to crow because I needed help.
I was sad. I was hungry. My feet hurt and
I was lonely. Today . . . I crow for JOY!
I was rescued! I feel loved. I am happy."

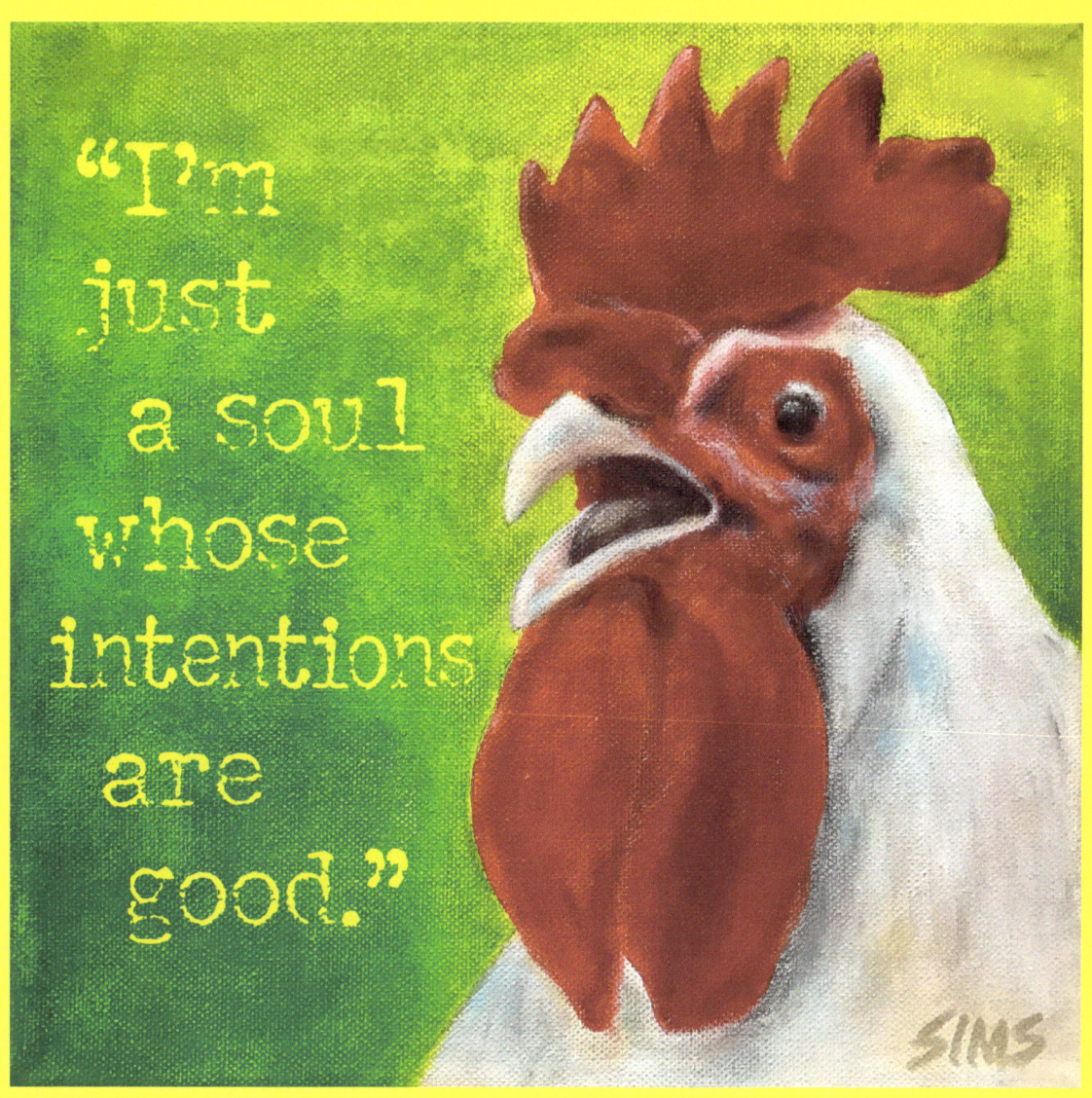

"At first, I didn't know what to do with so much space! There was a beautiful green pasture as far as I could see, and the biggest barn I ever saw! Inside was a warm and cozy stall filled with fresh straw, just for me. A tall horse and a baby pig came over to say hello. My first real home!"

Gratitude

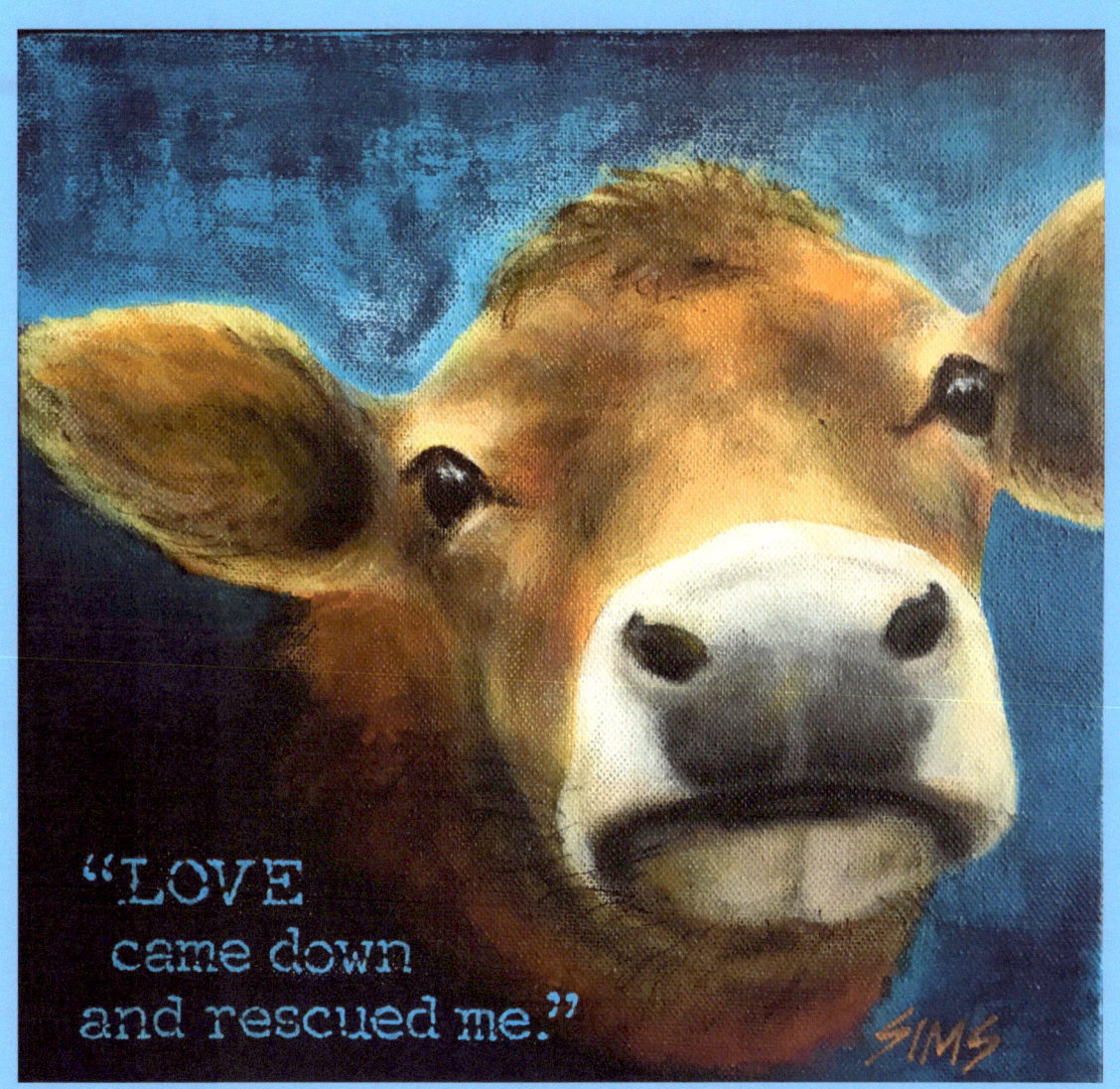

"LOVE came down and rescued me."

SIMS

"Our differences do not make us superior
or inferior; they just make us who we are.
That's it. Who you love does not matter to us.
All that matters is that you love. Love is
beautiful. Love is love."

Humanity

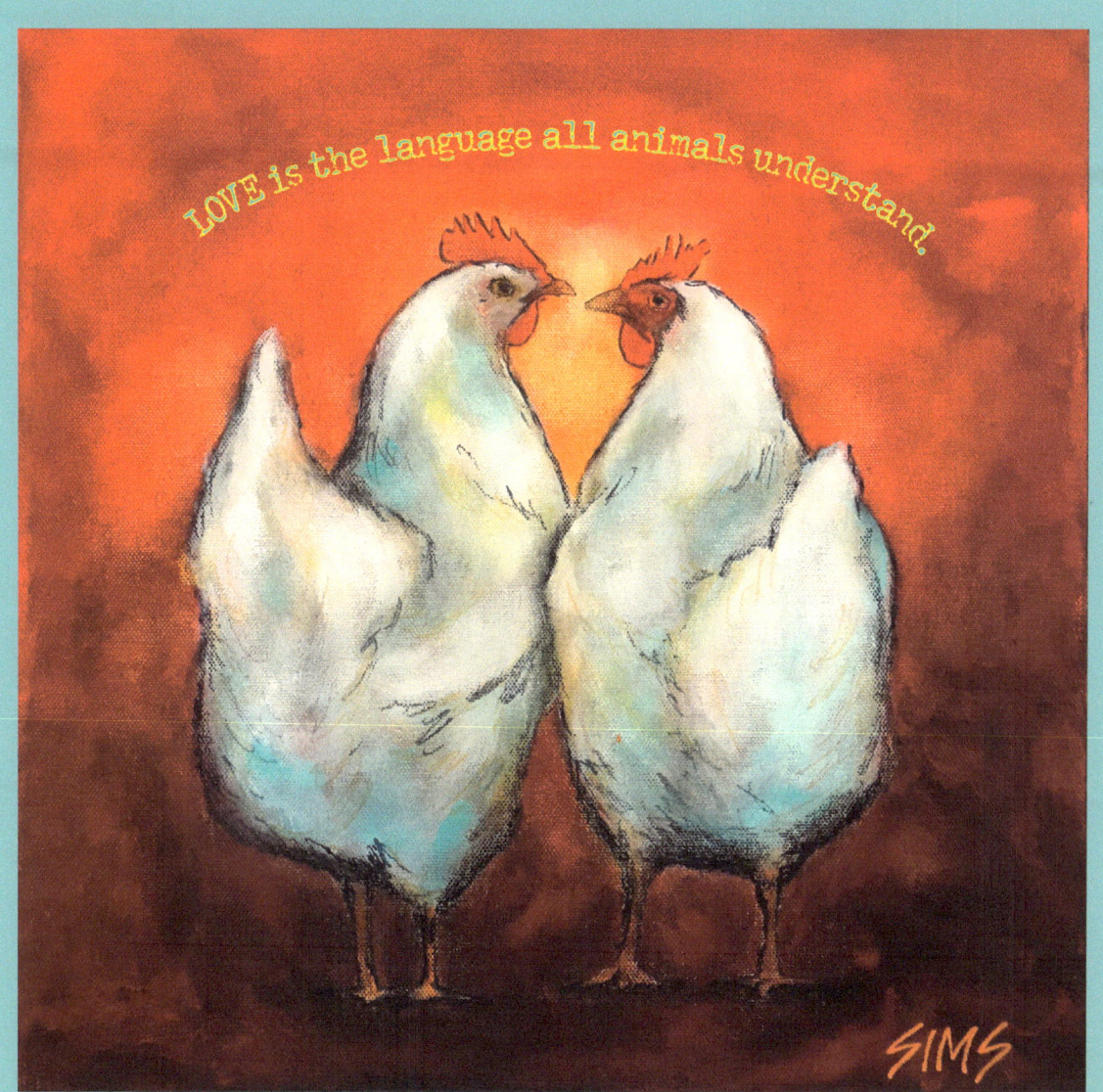

"My life didn't start out so well. But I have learned how to love and be loved, thanks to some caring humans who believed in me.
I hope others will give it a try!"

Courage

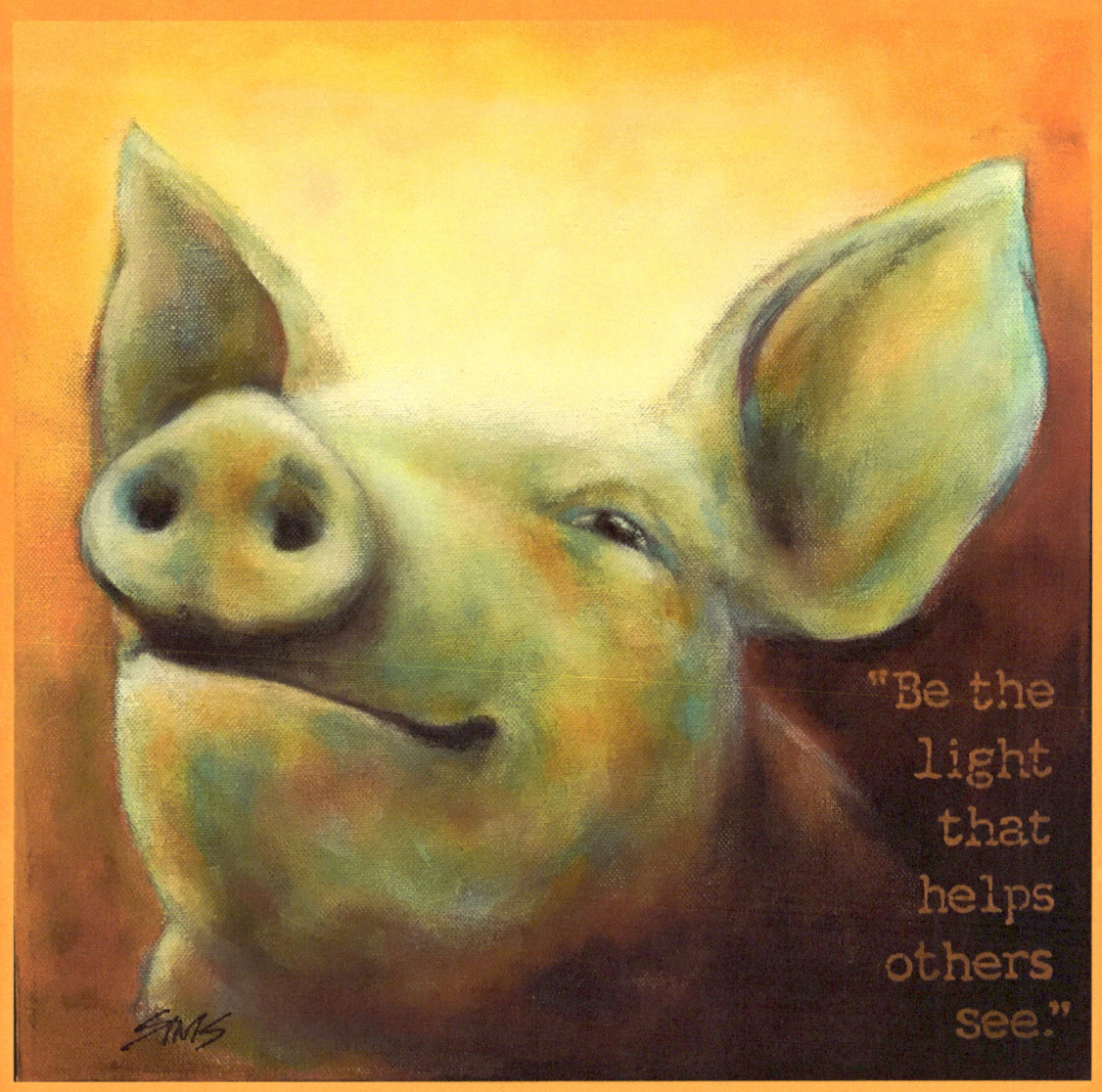

"Be the
light
that
helps
others
see."

"We all scattered when we heard the loud pops – firecrackers? After several days, I gave up hoping I'd find my family again. I thought my life was over. I fell asleep under an old truck. When I woke up, I was here! I don't mind living with humans – actually I prefer it, as long as I can be social and feel like part of the family. I am a lucky rabbit to be here. I am understood, loved, and part of this wonderful family."

Hope

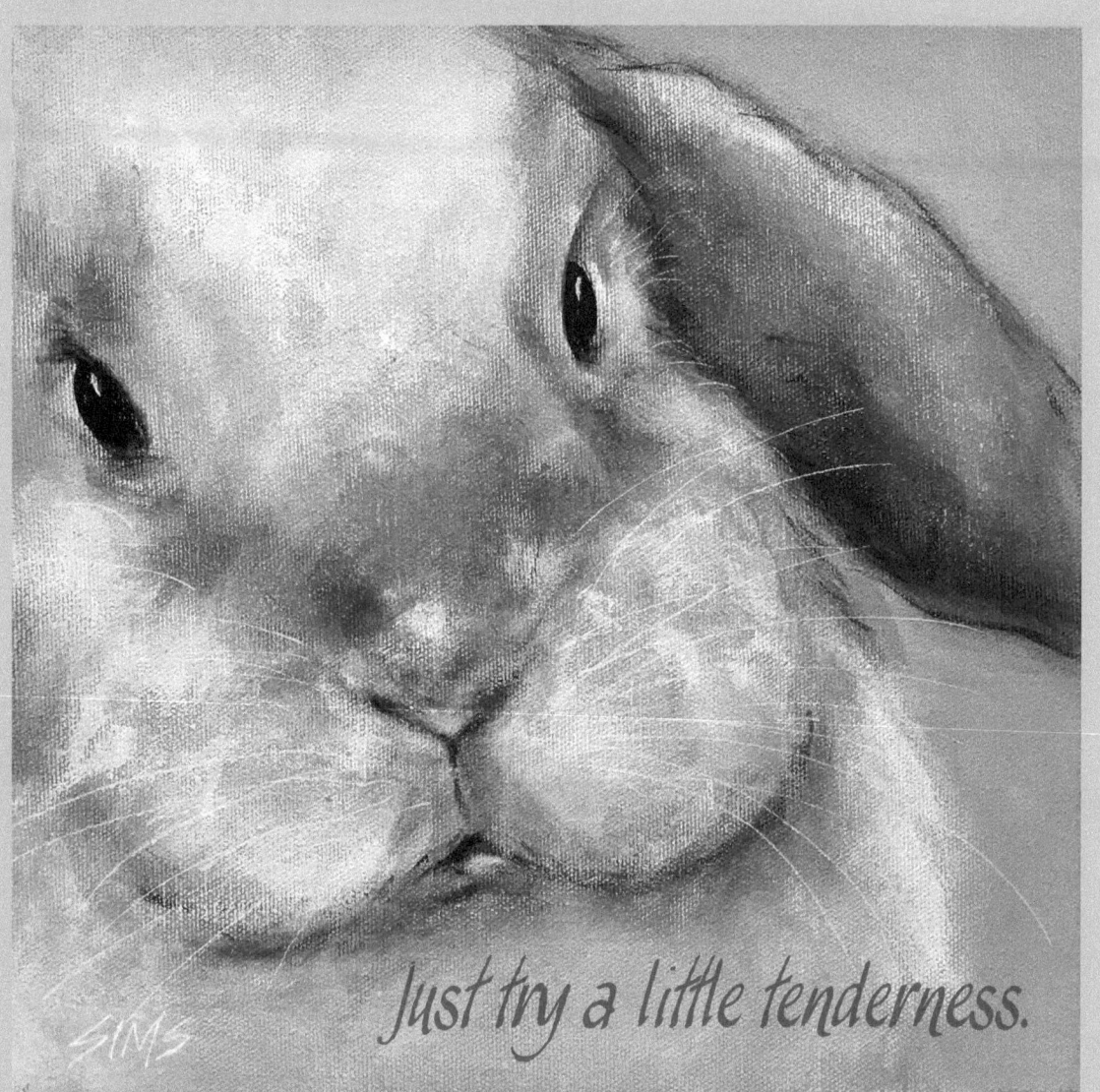

Just try a little tenderness.

SIMS

"Everyone who works here or volunteers to help us at this sanctuary is 'vegan.' I didn't know what that meant before I came here to live. Now I know that vegans are my BEST FRIENDS! They don't eat animals!"

Heart

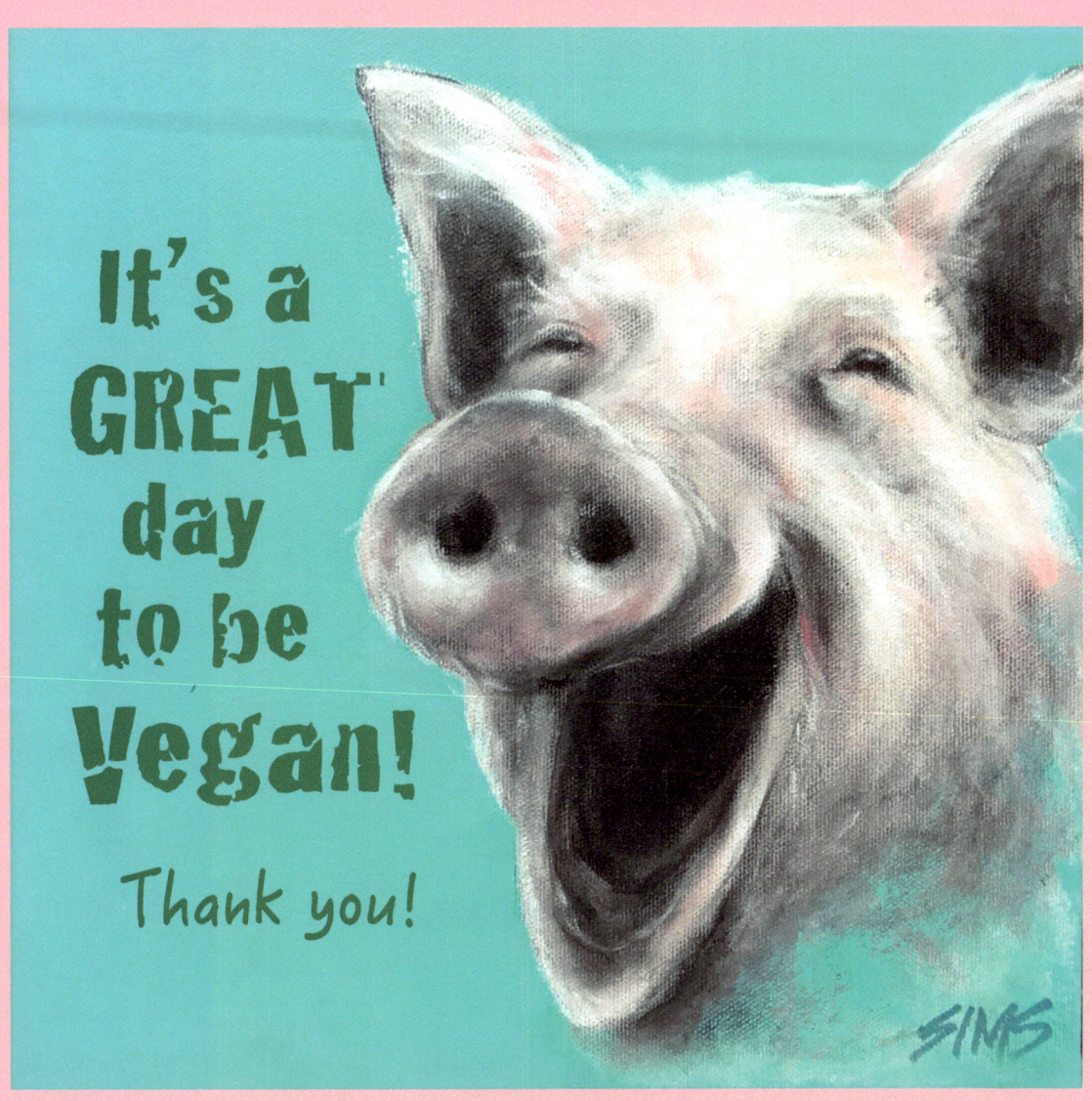

"Life took us to unexpected places . . .
LOVE brought us home."

Faith

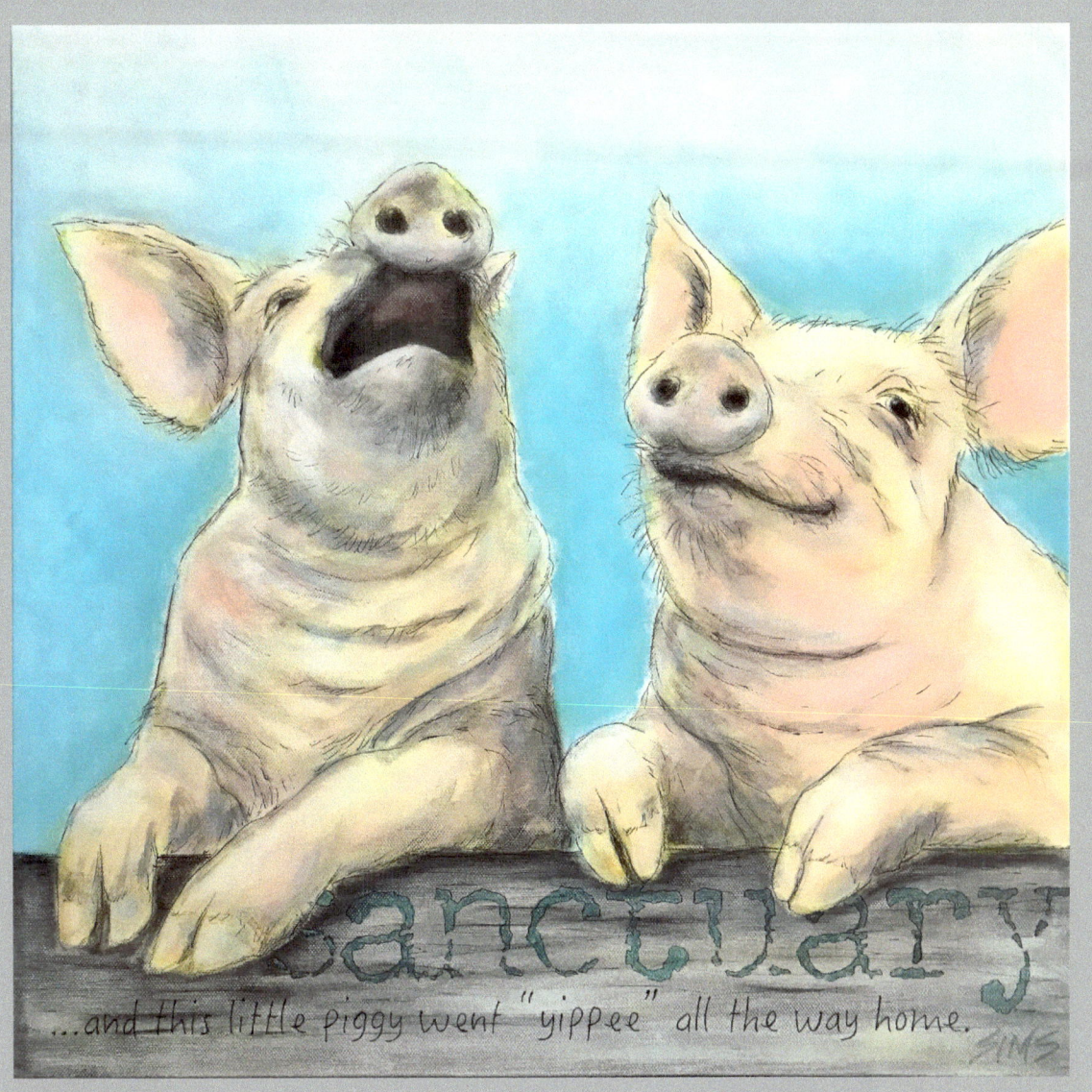

...and this little piggy went "yippee" all the way home.

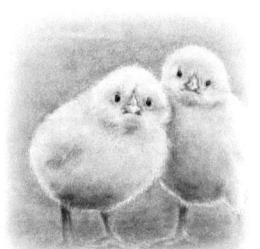

The Courage to LOVE

I'm not sure if it was a survival instinct or maybe a higher power at work . . . but whatever it was, I felt compelled to paint these animals and let their voices be heard.

Inspired by their will to live and their courage to love, trust, and forgive . . . I could feel my own life begin again. I started to see my new world as a sanctuary.

I believe what truly matters is how we treat each other; how we can provide sanctuary for those in need; and how we must share our stories so that others can learn and grow.

We ALL have the capacity to love.

We ALL can try to help each other find the courage to love.

We ALL deserve to be happy.

ALL of us.

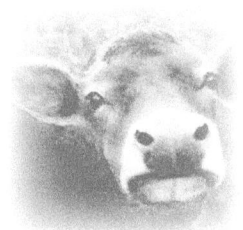

ACKNOWLEDGMENTS...

• Susanne, my partner in life. You opened my eyes to how a plant-based diet is good for my health, but most important how being vegan is vital to ending animal suffering.

• Leslie Naylor, one of the most dedicated animal advocates I know. Your invitation to hang my art in your restaurant ignited a spark in me that changed my life.

• My dear friends and fellow artists, Kathy McChesney and Pat Launer. You got me back on track when my story started to veer, and also made sure my grammar passed the test.

• To all who continue to support my life and my work. By purchasing my art and books, then posting nice things about them on Facebook to share with others, you give me the courage and confidence to keep going.

• All the vegans and animal advocates of the world! You will be on the right side of history when the day comes for all humans to acknowledge that a plant-based diet is better for your health, better for the planet, and absolutely vital to ending animal suffering.

ABOUT THE AUTHOR...

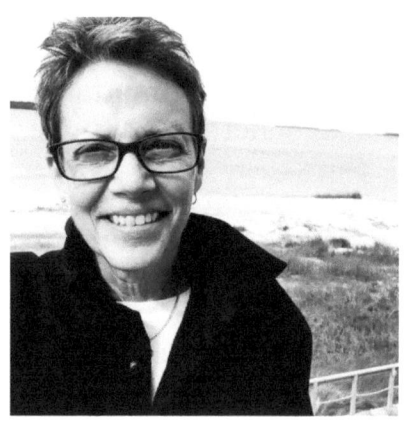

Jody Sims grew up in a small farming community in western Illinois, where she was greatly influenced by cartoons and the graphic art on cereal boxes. She studied fine art at Illinois State University in the 1970s, and then embarked on an extraordinary life as a graphic designer, illustrator, muralist, film producer, event planner, newspaper publisher, and community leader spanning 38 years in San Diego, California.

Jody became a vegetarian in 2012, shortly after she was diagnosed with breast cancer. It wasn't until 2015, after she and her spouse moved to Knoxville, Tennessee and met the animals at the Gentle Barn, that she became a vegan.

Jody is the author of *Soul Provider: Conversations With My Cat*, which showcases 20 of her original paintings of her cat's face, along with journal entries of her experience living through cancer. It won a Nautilus Book Award in 2014. In many ways, *Sanctuary* is a sequel to that book.

www.jodysims.com